BLUE-TONGUES IN GI

THE PAST AND THE FUTURE

Recently my wife purchased a pair of wild-caught New Guinea Blue-tongued Skinks, *Tiliqua gigas*. Though large, hardy, and attractive enough to draw interest, it has became obvious that their main attraction is their personality. These are big, active species have been bred in captivity and a very few are imported as wild-caught adults. For a quarter of a century Australia, the home of all the blue-tongue species but one or perhaps two, has been off-limits to reptile exportation, so the Australian species now in the

PHOTO BY K. H. SWITAK

Perhaps one of the most endearing qualities of the blue-tongued skinks is their tamability; many can be carried about or set in your lap. This canine- or feline-like affability makes them more "pet-like" than most other herptiles.

lizards that really seem to enjoy being handled and rapidly learned to recognize us. Even the household dogs and cats (hair and scales is almost always a dangerous combination) don't seem to phase them or make them nervous.

Traditionally all books that cover pet lizards have covered the blue-tongued skinks, and they have a long and fairly successful history in the hobby. Several hobby should in theory all be long-term captives and their offspring. (As we'll see, this may not always be the case—when dealing with expensive pets, some circumvention of the laws should be expected, though of course not condoned.) This limited availability has led to very high prices for specimens and thus a reduced likelihood that average hobbyists could afford to purchase pairs and breed them, leading to lower prices. Currently the blue-tongues are still show-stoppers and attention-getters at any herp expo and pet shop, and none really is inexpensive. However, the times they are a-changing, and more and more captive-breds seem to be available each autumn.

Just what are blue-tongues, how many species are there, and how do you successfully keep and breed these big, friendly lizards? I'll try to answer these questions in the following chapters, but expect many gaps in my coverage. The facts about identification and range and such are simple enough and very available, but information on captive-care of any but the most common species is either unpublished or I just couldn't find it during the research for this book. Additionally, new importations from Irian Jaya (Indonesian New Guinea) are starting to come in and present serious questions as to identification, relationships to Australian blue-tongues, and how sustainable these forms will be in the herpetocultural business. Blue-tongues are pets in a state of flux and still of undetermined futures. I hope they will become more common and affordable to the average hobbyist, because they certainly have many enjoyable features to make them among the best of all pet lizards.

More and more blue-tongued skink specimens are being imported to meet growing commercial demands. Unfortunately, the exact identity of such specimens sometimes is a mystery. This animal, for example, hails from the Tanimbar Islands (and thus is referred to as the Tanimbar Blue-tongued Skink), but exactly where it belongs in the taxonomic picture is unknown. Most believe it to be simply a variety of the Common Blue-tongued Skink, *Tiliqua scincoides*.

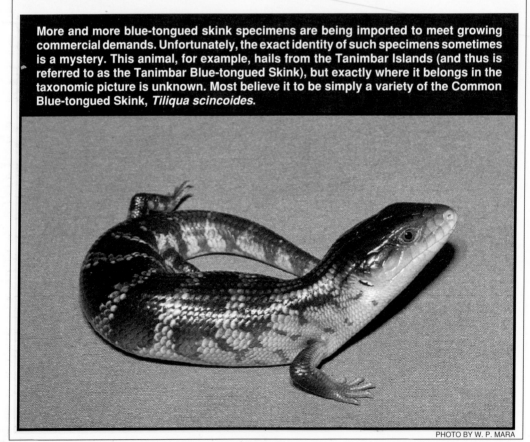

PHOTO BY W. P. MARA

PHOTO BY R. D. BARTLETT

Blue-tongued skinks are part of a very large family of lizards known as the Scincidae, which contains almost 100 genera and probably more than 1000 species.

WHAT ARE BLUE-TONGUES?

If you read my book *Skinks: Identification, Care & Breeding* (T.F.H., RE-111), you realize that the lizard family Scincidae is a gigantic one, with almost 100 genera and probably a 1000 species. Australia is the true Nirvana of Skinkdom, with over 30 genera and well over 360 species (with more described every year). Of these 360 species, only ten (plus one from Indonesia and New Guinea) are blue-tongues, formerly all placed in one genus, *Tiliqua*, described by the English naturalist Gray in 1825. Though these skinks share many structural and behavioral features (including all the species being viviparous or livebearing), they differ strikingly in others and fall into four well-defined groups that recently have been considered full genera. Though the status of these genera is somewhat controversial, I'm going to recognize them here because, frankly, I feel that they follow easily seen distinctions in body form and thus are recognizable by eye, as opposed to so many recently separated genera that can be recognized only by detailed anatomical studies or studies of the skeleton, chromosomes, or cellular chemistry.

First, the blue-tongues are lygosomine skinks, belonging to the same subfamily as most of the Australian skinks and many other species from around the world such as the Ground Skink, *Scincella lateralis*, of the United States. Within this gigantic subfamily they can be recognized by several details of head scalation (especially the failure of

One characteristic of the genus *Tiliqua* is the ear lobules that protect the tympanic cavity.

the paired parietal scales to touch behind the interparietal—the parietals are the three large scales on top of the head behind the eyes in normal skinks, the interparietal being the middle one of the three) and by foot structure. Hobbyists probably won't bother looking at head scales, but a look at the hind feet of a pet blue-tongue should be enlightening. In most skinks (and most lizards, for that matter), the toes are long and slender, the one on the inside of the foot (called the first toe) shortest and the third and fourth, especially the fourth, longest. In all the blue-tongues, the toes are relatively short and wide (probably an adaptation for a terrestrial, burrowing existence), with the third and fourth toes equal in length or the third actually a bit longer than the fourth. The closest relatives of the blue-tongues appear to be the skinks of the genus *Egernia*, also very well-represented in Australia and with a few species in the herp hobby. *Egernia* species have the toes of the hind feet normal for skinks, the fourth toe longer than the third and much longer than the other toes. In most blue-tongues the scales tend to be smooth and polished (though at least some male New Guinea Blue-tongues, *Tiliqua gigas*, have strong folds or radiating lines on the head and some body scales, and the Shingleback, *Trachydosaurus*, is notoriously rough-scaled), while in *Egernia* in the hobby the scales of at least the tail are spiny. Not all blue-tongues have blue tongues, but most have large, brightly colored tongues that are displayed during combat and when threatened by a potential predator.

The blue-tongues fall into four groups of species with obviously different body shapes and some structural characters to back up the habitus (an old word for general appearance or shape) differences. Thus today we recognize four genera of blue-tongues as follows:

Genus *Cyclodomorphus* was described by Fitzinger in 1843 and includes slender, rather small species with simple color patterns and tails that if complete are about as long as (and sometimes longer than) the distance from the tip of the snout to the vent or cloaca (the snout-vent length, SVL, so often used in technical lizard descriptions). The legs often are very short, even for a blue-tongue. The heads of the species are rather narrow, not markedly set off from the body by a more slender neck as in all the other blue-tongues. For a while these species were put in a genus called *Omolepida*, but it appears that *Cyclodomorphus* is older and the correct name for the genus.

Genus *Hemisphaeriodon* was coined in 1867 by Peters to include the Pink-tongued Skink, still its only species. Like *Cyclodomorphus*, *Hemisphaeriodon* is relatively slender and has a tail that is at least as long as the snout-vent length. However, the head is broad and set off from the body by an obvious neck. Unlike the

Notice the toe length of this blue-tongue specimen—the third toe is slightly longer than the fourth. This seemingly insignificant characteristic is in fact a diagnostic feature of the genus *Tiliqua*, since most other skinks have a long *fourth* toe rather than a third.

PHOTO BY MALETA AND JERRY G. WALLS

Cyclodomorphus species, the legs are long and strong, fitting for the arboreal lifestyle of the Pink-tongue. There are some scale count differences between the two genera, especially number of scales around the body near the middle (30 to 34 in *Hemisphaeriodon*, 20 to 28 in *Cyclodomorphus*), but just general body form and color patterns are sufficient to distinguish these genera from each other and from the other blue-tongues. *Hemisphaeriodon* often is included within *Cyclodomorphus* by taxonomists.

The true blue-tongues, genus *Tiliqua* (described by Gray in 1825), are bizarre but often beautiful skinks with very short toes on the hind feet and short tails. In no species is the tail much more than half to three-quarters the snout-vent length (though I have to admit that the tails of *T. gigas* and *T. scincoides* often appear longer than they really are if you were to measure them and often appear to be as long as the body without the head), and the head is broad compared to the slender neck. The scales are smooth or nearly so, never knobby or spiny. Technically, the scales under the toes of the hind feet (the digital lamellae of the taxonomist) are not divided. This is the only genus that occurs outside Australia and is the most common in herpetoculture, with about four species currently available if you have the money and patience to track them down.

Lastly we have the unique Shinglebacks or Bobtails, genus *Trachydosaurus*, perhaps the

The taxonomy of the Pink-tongued Skink always seems to be in debate. Some workers place it in the monotypic genus *Hemisphaeriodon* (species name *gerrardi*), others put it in *Cyclodomorphus*, while still others think it belongs in *Tiliqua* with many other close relatives of that genus.

PHOTO BY K. H. SWITAK

The Shinglebacks, *Trachydosaurus rugosus*, often are synonymized with the blue-tongues in spite of obvious external morphological differences. Shinglebacks are calm, resigning creatures that often occur in colonies.

most instantly recognizable lizards. This genus also was described by Gray back in 1825, but it has had a checkered history, often being synonymized with *Tiliqua* regardless of great external differences in body form. In the Bobtails the tail is very short, only a quarter or so of the snout-vent length, broad, and blunt (though admittedly quite variable), sometimes resembling a second head. The scales are enlarged and knobby, often rather spiny, giving the animal the appearance of a pinecone. The scales on the head are variously broken up and irregular and no longer can be clearly identified with the particular scales of *Tiliqua*. Technically, the digital lamellae of the hind toes are divided or split, a feature that certainly doesn't seem to be essential for recognizing the distinctiveness of this genus. These are peaceful, colonial lizards that may be very abundant in parts of Australia but are extremely rare in the hobby at the moment and command very high prices.

AVAILABILITY

Currently there are 11 recognized species of blue-tongues plus four more subspecies, for a total of 15 nameable blue-tongues. Of this small number, seven or eight are regularly seen in the herpetocultural market, but only four (*Hemisphaeriodon gerrardi, Tiliqua gigas, T. scincoides scincoides, T. scincoides intermedia*) are likely to be available without either large bank accounts or several years of

Shown is a beautiful neonatal example of a blue-tongued skink. As with most other herptiles, it is preferable to purchase a blue-tongue at such a young age. Photo by R. D. Bartlett.

searching. Fortunately, all four of these make excellent pets, are large, and can be purchased for less than a month's salary. Also, these four species all have distinctive color patterns and are easy to identify, though some dealers still seem to get them mixed up a bit. Only *Tiliqua gigas* still is imported as wild-caught adults, but today it is being bred in small numbers and the future looks bright for an increasing abundance of captive-bred babies in the coming years.

When purchasing any blue-tongue, be sure you get a healthy, active specimen. Because of the cost of these pets, it would be best to have a veterinarian check the specimen over, looking especially for intestinal parasites, which sometimes can be a problem. Try to get specimens without scars or missing toes (captive-bred babies should be perfect), but as we will see, adult females go through very rough mating behaviors and often become scarred or lose a toe as a normal aspect of their lives. Look for non-aggressive animals that respond well to handling. Unlike many other lizards, blue-tongues *must* be handled often to reveal their personality, and they are strong enough to take handling without problems. Large adults (often over 15 inches long) can have painful bites, and you don't want to get on their bad side. Since babies of almost all the species are 4 to 6 inches long at birth, they seldom are a problem to maintain.

OK, so much for the introduction. Now on to the real fun of keeping and breeding these fantastic lizards.

There are plenty of captive-bred blue-tongued skinks available to interested hobbyists. If possible, get yourself a captive-bred specimen over one that has been taken from the wild. In truth, only the New Guinea Blue-tongued Skink, *Tiliqua gigas*, still is collected with any regularity.

PHOTO BY R. D. BARTLETT

KEEPING BLUE-TONGUES

Because of their large adult size, the available blue-tongues usually are easy to maintain in captivity, though their size itself is a source of problems. Keeping blue-tongues can be a simple task once their terraria are set up correctly and you develop a depends on what species is available to you when you go lizard shopping and how much money you have in your hobby fund. Remember, we are dealing with expensive lizards here—there are no cheap blue-tongues at the moment, though growing

Keeping blue-tongued skinks is relatively easy once you get your specimens settled into a properly equipped enclosure and on a feeding regimen. The only real advantage to obtaining adult specimens over newborns is that they can be bred more or less right away.

PHOTO OF *HEMISPHAERIODON GERRARDI* BY R. D. BARTLETT

suitable feeding regimen. Here we'll discuss the keeping of the common *Tiliqua* species in some detail. Differences, where they exist, in keeping oak skinks, Pink-tongues, and Shinglebacks will be mentioned under those species.

BABY OR ADULT?

First you have to buy your blue-tongue. Should you get a cute baby only a few weeks or months old or an established adult? To some extent the answer enthusiasm and successes in captive-breeding are sure to lead to increased availability and lower prices.

Even baby blue-tongues are large lizards compared to the average pet shop anole or swift. They have large appetites and grow extremely fast. Because babies are nippy with each other, they should be housed individually in 10-gallon or larger terraria. Their colors are bright, their personalities can be developed through regular handling, and they are tough.

However, they have at least one major drawback: they need tremendous amounts of calcium supplementation (as well as vitamins) during their period of active growth. Breeders report that babies can grow so fast that their bones literally do not keep up with muscle growth and they die as collapsed bags of flesh. Don't let this happen to your baby! Additionally, baby blue-tongues need temperatures about 4 to 5°F higher than adults of the same species, as a general rule.

Adults, on the other hand, immediately need large quarters, which makes them more expensive to house. Their colors are duller than those of babies, and they are generally more expensive than babies. (Wild-caught imported New Guinea and Irian Jaya Blue-tongues are exceptions in that adults are relatively cheaper than the few available captive-bred babies.) Adults often are missing toes, may have partially regenerated tails, and usually are scarred to some extent. Adults are closer to breeding age, obviously an advantage if you are considering captive-breeding. Adults may not have been handled on a regular basis and may have "rough" personalities for a while until they get used to being picked up every day. Big blue-tongues have heavy jaw muscles and large teeth, and they hurt.

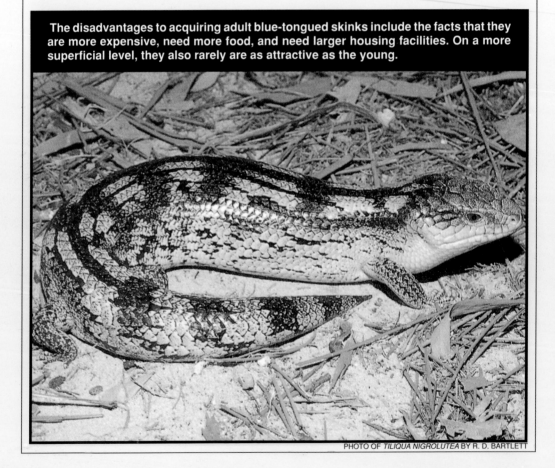

The disadvantages to acquiring adult blue-tongued skinks include the facts that they are more expensive, need more food, and need larger housing facilities. On a more superficial level, they also rarely are as attractive as the young.

PHOTO OF *TILIQUA NIGROLUTEA* BY R. D. BARTLETT

Any newly acquired blue-tongued skink that was collected in the wild should be brought to a veterinarian for an initial checkup. Chances are it will have intestinal parasites and need deworming. A brief period of quarantine also is strongly urged.

PHOTO BY ISABELLE FRANCAIS

GENERAL HEALTH

Blue-tongues are robust, hardy lizards with relatively few ills. If caged in large terraria, fed correctly, and kept warm, they will live for years. Like all lizards, however, they are subject to parasites of various types and also have accidents.

First, get your blue-tongue vetted. If wild-collected, it will have intestinal parasites and must be wormed by a competent veterinarian. Many pet shops that sell these expensive lizards have already protected their investment by having the animals wormed the day they enter the shop, and they will be glad to provide proof of this. You should have a vet on call anyway, just in case.

Mites, mouthrot, and other typical lizard diseases can occur in blue-tongues but are not common. Your vet will show you how to treat such problems; blue-tongues are too expensive to risk treating with home remedies in most cases.

They also are subject to shedding problems, partially because their fast growth leads to almost perpetual shedding. In blue-tongues the skin peels off in small pieces, some of which may not loosen from the toes in time to prevent constriction problems. Blue-tongues have small, rather fragile toes that should be checked on a regular basis. Few blue-tongues like to soak for any length of time, and it may be necessary to force-soak a lizard every month or two to help loosen any adhering bits of skin. Also, watch out for bits of substrate wedged under chin scales. A bit of sand or peat moss under a scale interferes with molting to some extent and could cause ever-growing problems with each shed. Cleaning such an inclusion with hydrogen peroxide on a cotton-tipped swab should prevent problems.

Blue-tongues often display a claw that is much larger than the others and twisted. I guess such an overgrown claw probably will not cause major problems, but it is worrisome. Your vet may recommend a simple snip to remove the claw. Any bleeding can be controlled with hydrogen peroxide.

Female blue-tongues of breeding age will be scarred. There is no way around this, because mating is vigorous in these species, with the male grabbing the female by her nape, side, or leg during breeding fights. Occasionally a toe is pulled or twisted off as well. Biting usually causes minor bleeding but apparently no major discomfort to the female. Swab the wound down with hydrogen peroxide and apply a bit of antibiotic salve (available from your veterinarian) to ensure that there are no secondary infections. Try to keep the female clean until the abraded area

heals, but generally there will be more mating bouts and the female will have to be pretty much on her own. If well-fed and warm, there should be no problems other than minor scars.

THE TERRARIUM

If you have a baby blue-tongue, anywhere from 5 to 10 inches long, it can be kept in the standard all-glass 10-gallon tank (20 X 12 X 10 inches), but giving it a 20-gallon long (30 X 12 X 12 inches) will give it room to grow and hold off buying a larger cage for a few more months. These skinks grow very fast, and within the year you will be dealing with a lizard that is over a foot long and in need of larger accommodations. Baby blue-tongues are best kept separately to prevent fights, allow individual checking of feeding, and promote regular handling.

Adult blue-tongues need at least a 50-gallon terrarium and would prefer a 3 X 5 ft enclosure if possible. They need floor space, not height, so most commercial terraria are just shaped wrong. If you have a secure herp-room, you could

PHOTO COURTESY OF CORALIFE/ENERGY SAVERS

Organic substrates work well with blue-tongued skinks. They can be purchased in bulk quantities, are easy to work with, and are highly absorbent.

entire terrarium and its contents should be carefully cleaned each week.

OUTDOOR ACCOMMODATIONS

If you are one of the lucky people who lives in a climate that is warm and (preferably) relatively dry most of the year, you can consider establishing your blue-tongues in a shed or greenhouse. This will give them sufficient space to move around and behave normally (in nature blue-tongues are sedentary and seldom travel far from where they were born) while requiring minimal cleaning and maintenance time from the keeper. Blue-tongues also breed

Under-tank heating pads work well with blue-tongues. They will warm only one particular section of the enclosure, giving the inmate(s) more than one temperature zone to choose from.

Keeping an eye on the air temperature of your blue-tongued skink's enclosure is an important facet of good husbandry. If the animal is allowed to become too warm or too cold, it could become ill. Fortunately, high-range thermometers designed specifically for herp-keeping now are available.

well in such surroundings, probably because the males can freely follow selected females around for several days as they would in nature. Just be sure that the bottom of the outdoor enclosure is securely screened for several inches into the ground so the lizards cannot dig out. If you provide a maze of PVC tubing partially buried in the ground, the lizards will really feel at home.

Remember that dogs, cats, rats, hawks, and various other predators (including humans of various ages and desires) are more likely to notice blue-tongues kept outside. Predators such as dogs can be kept out easily enough with simple latches, but humans may require more extensive locks and precautions. Blue-tongues are valuable commodities, and thefts are not uncommon. Insurance seldom protects the value of pet lizards. It might be best to keep your hobby in the background and not blatantly let strangers know about what you are keeping.

HEATING

Blue-tongues require two types of heating in their terrarium. First, they need basking lights in a corner of the terrarium, preferably focused on flat rocks or ceramic plates. The normal activity pattern of a blue-tongue is to awake, shuffle into the sun (i.e., basking light), warm up to 85 to 95°F, and then more rapidly move away from the heat and assume feeding and other activities. The basking lights help bring them up to active temperature rapidly and naturally. An undertank heating pad near the basking lights will maintain a temperature of at least 80°F in its vicinity, and lizards often will bury themselves near it on cooler nights or even during the day if they want warmth without light. The far end of the terrarium must always be unheated so the skinks can cool down sufficiently (often as low as 65°F is tolerated) at night. Be sure that a hide box or tube is in this cool area.

LIGHTING

As diurnal lizards, blue-tongues like the light and they are used to basking in sunlight.

Their heavy scales prevent much ultraviolet absorption, however. Most keepers like to provide the skinks with fluorescent lights made specifically for reptiles and providing a good balance of visible light and ultraviolet. Such lights are easy to find in your local pet shop. The ballasts of fluorescents also provide a little bit of extra heat and ensure that the air as well as the substrate is warm. Lights must of course be kept above the terrarium and shine in through screening because glass absorbs most of the ultraviolet.

That's it. As along as the terrarium is large enough to accommodate your pet or pets, properly heated, and well-lighted, as well as supplied with hide boxes, you should have no problems keeping blue-tongues securely and healthfully. Remember that these are big, sometimes aggressive lizards that will fight among themselves, so never put more than two adults in a 50-gallon terrarium or one baby in a 20-gallon or smaller tank. Unlike most lizards, blue-tongues should be handled on a daily basis if at all possible, so their housing should be easy to get into. If you keep your blue-tongues outdoors, expect them to be a bit wilder than indoor pets.

Of course, to have really healthy skinks you have to feed them well. Because blue-tongues are a bit different in diet requirements from more common lizards, we'll have to treat feeding in some detail in the next chapter.

FEEDING BLUE-TONGUES

FEEDING REGIMENS

In nature the blue-tongues are omnivores, eating both plant and animal material. Most seem to be true generalists when it comes to feeding, taking what they can get. Because of the sedentary nature of adult blue-tongues and their tendency to form colonies of a sort, they seldom are active hunters, instead preferring slow-moving invertebrates and the fruits and flowers that occur in their territory. In captivity the blue-tongues tend to be very much individuals, in keeping with their "high intelligence" compared to most lizards, and specimens have definite likes and dislikes that may make feeding difficult. No blue-tongue will starve if food is available, but they certainly can make their keeper worry.

Blue-tongues feed when the lights are on and their body temperature has risen to the proper level for activity and digestion, usually over 80°F and in some forms as much as 95°F. Babies need to be warmer than adults to digest their food properly, something to keep in mind. Babies also grow so fast that for the first six months or even a year you can almost literally see them get fractions of an inch longer each day. Unlike adults, which need vitamin and

PHOTO BY SUZANNE L. AND JOSEPH T. COLLINS

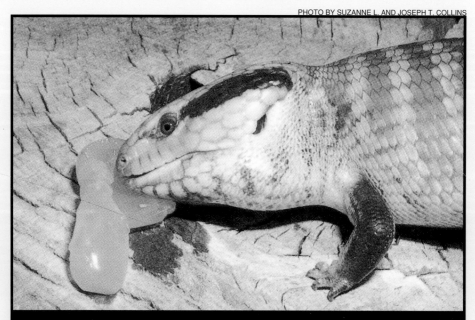

Although blue-tongued skinks are considered omnivorous, exact feeding habits largely are a matter of individual preference. The best approach a keeper can take simply is to try different items with each specimen being kept.

calcium supplements (specifically designed for reptiles, of course) only once a week, every meal for a growing baby skink should be dosed with an appropriate calcium supplement and vitamins should be given every other meal.

Young blue-tongues should be fed every day at first, gradually after six months reducing feedings to every other day. This schedule can be kept up through

more often should be better than large meals rarely because this is the natural feeding behavior of skinks in the wild.

WATER

Every blue-tongue terrarium must have a dish of water. These skinks drink often and deeply if given the chance. Though the desert species probably seldom see free water, instead licking

Calcium additives, usually offered in powder form, now are available in most herp-oriented pet shops. It is ideal to sprinkle such powder onto a blue-tongue's foodstuffs (a practice often referred to as "dusting") at least once a week.

the life of the lizard, though some keepers insist that the adult skinks need food only once a week. Frankly, these lizards are much like cats when it comes to feeding time—they stare and work on your mind until you feed them. I can't imagine being stared at by an 18-inch lizard for seven days until the next meal, so it might be best to surrender to the inevitable and feed every other day. Unless the pet becomes obviously obese there is no harm. Small meals

condensation from rocks and leaves, they are quick to adapt to water on demand. Most blue-tongues are not especially likely to bathe and defecate in their water dish, but it is best to keep the dish small, cleaning it and replacing the water each day. The dish must be sturdy, with a wide base to stay upright when the lizards climb over it. Misting blue-tongues probably is not necessary but might make molting a bit easier and prevent problems.

PHOTO BY ISABELLE FRANCAIS

Small mice offer blue-tongued skinks a nutritious meal. Mice can be bought in quantity either live or, for greater convenience, pre-killed and frozen.

DOG FOOD PROS AND CONS

The easiest blue-tongue food to obtain and feed certainly is a good grade of dog food or cat food. A tremendous variety of nutritious brands is available, and one can may last several weeks if refrigerated. Low-fat types, designed for older or less active cats and dogs, may be best because of lower protein content. However, I've never seen a paper on just how much protein is needed by a blue-tongue skink, so worries about the problem of too much protein in a skink's diet may be completely without foundation. The argument is that most vegetarian or omnivorous reptiles suffer kidney problems if given diets too high in protein. Eventually the kidneys enlarge and deposits block the tubules, leading to systemic poisoning and death or at least a shorter lifetime. Blue-

There are many products designed to aid you with your reptile-keeping efforts, including sprays that loosen patches of unshed skin and liquid vitamins that can be sprayed directly onto all food items.

PHOTO COURTESY OF CORALIFE/ENERGY SAVERS

Snails seem to be relished by most blue-tongued skinks. Although snails provide good nutrition, they may be difficult for the average keeper to acquire on a regular basis.

tongues, however, definitely take animal prey in nature, and some keepers have succeeded admirably with diets based on animal flesh with only occasional vegetable supplements. Additionally, zoos have successfully kept and bred blue-tongues on artificial diets based on beef heart with exacting amounts of chemical supplements to provide the essential vitamins and minerals.

Perhaps a compromise is the best bet. A half teaspoon of high-quality dog food (I personally believe that most cat foods must have too much protein for safety, but other keepers adamantly disagree and say that cat food is fine) mushed with peas, grated carrots, diced zucchini, etc., given every other day could form the basic diet. Veggie salad should also be given on a regular basis. As long as the blue-tongue is feeding

actively and is healthy, without problems, and especially if it breeds, the diet has to be at least adequate.

Oh yes—dog food tends to dry on the edges of the mouth and could cause scale deformities with the next shed if allowed to remain. Since you should be handling your skink every day, take a second to clean its mouth after every meal. At least you don't have to brush its teeth!

VEGGIES

Everyone agrees that blue-tongues must have vegetables in their diet, and many keepers would suggest that adults will live on an all-veggie diet. Unfortunately, some skinks don't believe this and refuse to eat their veggies on a regular basis. Since keepers have kept blue-tongues for years strictly on canned cat and dog food and they reproduced and remained healthy, it probably is best not to stress the pet by forcing it to eat what it doesn't like.

However, it doesn't hurt to always give some veggies and fruit with each meal even for confirmed meat-eaters. Try mixing finely minced zucchini, apple, pear, melon, grapes, peas, spinach, and just about any other sweet fruit and green or yellow vegetable in with the canned food. Perhaps a vegetable puree or apple butter soaked into the meat will be taken without complaints. Some blue-tongues like flower petals, so in season try presenting them with roses, carnations, dandelions, and similar flowers, making sure, of course, that the flowers do not

A variety of vegetables should be offered to captive blue-tongued skinks, and the greater the variety the better. Also, the "veggie mix" should include some kind of vitamin supplement.

come from areas where herbicides and insecticides are used. A vitamin and mineral supplement once a week should give adult lizards sufficient trace nutrients even if they will not take vegetables. Of course, if the lizard likes veggie salad, give as much as it will eat with each feeding.

CRICKETS, ET AL.

When it comes to live foods, blue-tongues tend to be lazy feeders. Though many will track down and catch crickets and grasshoppers, others ignore crawling insects even if crickets perch on their snouts. Try giving babies gut-loaded crickets on a regular basis; if a lizard gets used to such food as a baby the taste may linger into adulthood.

Waxworms have an unusual smell that turns off some keepers and some blue-tongues, but some blue-tongues love them. Waxworms, like crickets, have the advantage of being easy to purchase and store all year; a trip to the local pet shop will give you food for several weeks. Mealworms also fit into this category, but we'll talk about them separately a bit later. Recently a type of giant waxworm, the so-called butterworm, has become available and is quite acceptable to many blue-tongues. This large caterpillar is the larva of the tropical American moth *Chilecomadia moorei*, a wood-borer. Little has been published on raising this moth in the home and it still is quite expensive compared to more usual foods, but it seems to be nutritious.

Many adult blue-tongues will take pinkie mice on occasion, and it is likely that they do occasionally run across similar nestlings in nature. Pinkies are an excellent source of calcium and a complete meal in a skin, so see if your blue-tongue will take pinkies (especially frozen and thoroughly thawed) as a treat. Large blue-tongues may take fuzzies and hoppers (older baby mice) as well.

A blue-tongued skink maintained on a carefully formulated diet will, in time, look as beautiful as this stunning New Guinea specimen. It is important to remember that all captive herptiles are solely dependent on their keeper for their well-being. It is a responsibility that shouldn't be taken casually. Photo by R. D. Bartlett.

Crickets probably are the food item most often offered to insectivorous herptiles. Crickets can be purchased at virtually any pet shop, in bulk, and in a variety of sizes.

Snails of all reasonable sizes are relished by most blue-tongues. It is amazing how even adult blue-tongues will gorge themselves on snails less than an eighth of an inch in diameter. Few people can culture snails successfully, so you will be dependent on wild-taken snails. Just be careful that you lift logs and dig through leaf litter only where no insecticides and herbicides have been applied for several years. The thin-shelled brownish aquatic snails (mostly *Physa* and *Lymnaea* species) often sold in pet shops or found as contaminants in clumps of aquatic plants live for hours or days outside the water and may be an excellent treat for your blue-tongues. As with any wild-caught food, however, they may carry parasites, though it is unlikely that non-Australian snails would have anything that could live for long in a blue-tongue. Some keepers have reported large masses of crushed snail shell being passed by their lizards and worry that impactions might occur if too many snails are fed. It seems more likely that a healthy, warm blue-tongue would absorb calcium from the shells before they could harden into an impassable mass. Small slugs also will be taken by some blue-tongues, but most species you run across in the back yard will be awfully slimy.

GIANT MEALWORMS

The Common Mealworm, *Tenebrio molitor*, has been a mainstay of herp diets for years, and it certainly will be taken by many blue-tongues. However, the Giant Mealworm recently has entered the pet shops in numbers and appears to be an even better food for blue-tongues. Baby blue-tongues often will take Giant Mealworms at every meal, though it seems likely that too many mealworms could cause gut impaction and chemical imbalances (mealworms are very high in phosphorus but low in calcium).

The Giant Mealworm is properly known as *Zophobas atratus*. Any other spelling or specific name you have seen is currently incorrect. This species is a large black beetle that in nature is especially common in caves, where the larvae feed in deposits of bat guano. It also may occur in detritus piles and other organic waste. The species was first cultured in the laboratory about 1965 by Dr. Walter Tschinkel, who has studied its behavior in great detail.

Like the Common Mealworm, *Zophobas atratus* larvae feed well on bran flakes, oatmeal, chicken mash, and similar bedding materials. The larvae are large, sometimes more than one gram in weight, and relatively thin-shelled compared to the regular mealworm. Many keepers swear by them because they provide more digestible contents relative to cuticle (shell) weight than smaller mealworms. Unfortunately, it may be hard to maintain breeding colonies in the home because the larvae are very cannibalistic and tend to disperse before they pupate. If not allowed to separate themselves from the mass of the larvae, older larvae use up their

Mealworms don't offer complete nutrition to blue-tongued skinks, but they do make a great supplementary food. Like crickets, they can be purchased at many pet shops and are not difficult to maintain once you get them home.

stored body fats without maturing and eventually die as almost empty shells. Also, larvae will eat pupae that do form in the culture and are not isolated. Success usually requires transferring the largest larvae to individual small plastic cups with a minimum of food until they pupate and eventually mature into adults. The Giant Mealworm needs a bit warmer temperatures than the Common Mealworm; some breeders keep the cultures over the fluorescent lights of the terrarium for extra heat.

"Gut loading" is the practice of giving high-vitamin meals to your blue-tongued skink's livefood items in the hopes that those vitamins will be passed on to your skinks when the livefood items are eaten.

PHOTO BY ISABELLE FRANCAIS

BREEDING BLUE-TONGUES

All the blue-tongued skinks are livebearers; the eggs are matured inside the mother and fully formed, active young are delivered. From birth the young are independent, though in natural situations they usually stay close to the mother for several months or possibly years. Since all the blue-tongues are from areas south of the Equator, they breed in response to reversed seasons, their summer being our winter, etc. Most of the species, including some of the common ones, come from areas with quite cold winters and are not really tropical animals. To breed blue-tongues you have to adjust them to Northern Hemisphere seasons. This is best done by a cooling period.

PHOTO BY R. D. BARTLETT

Many herptiles are bred in albino forms and their offspring regularly sold in the pet trade. Not the blue-tongues, however. At the moment, albino specimens are ultra-rare.

COOLING

Though typical blue-tongues grow fast, it seems that they are not sexually mature until at least two years old, probably closer to three years. Breeding skinks younger than this probably is futile and will just lead to fights and no young. When your blue-tongues are fully grown for the species, healthy, and (you hope) at least two years old, spend the summer and autumn months feeding them up, making sure they have plenty of fat in the tail base and good muscles on the legs. In November begin to reduce the terrarium temperature, hours of light, and food. By the end of November the cage should reach only 70°F during the day, with no more than eight hours of light (preferably less). Night temperatures of 60°F are preferred. Species from southern and eastern Australia should have somewhat lower temperatures (high of 65°F, low about 55°F) than the more tropical New Guinea and northern Australia species and subspecies. The lizards should be cool enough to become inactive and stop eating. Always keep water in the cage, as they will drink occasionally on warm days.

Keep the blue-tongues under these conditions for at least two months, then slowly bring them out with increasing heat, longer hours of light, and water baths to flush out the kidneys and gut. Within a week the skinks should be feeding normally and, you hope, ready to breed. It is best to house the specimens separately during the recovery period after cooling.

Not everyone agrees that a cooling period is necessary for successful breeding, and I know that wild-caught adult New Guinea heavier jowls, and a broader tail base (for the hemipenes) on a somewhat longer (or shorter!) tail as male characters, but none of these hold up perfectly in practice. Probing does not work on blue-tongues (the differences in probe depth between the sexes are very small and variable with size of the animal), and exposing the hemipenes by slowly and carefully rolling the thumb along the tail toward the vent only works reliably

"Popping" the hemipenes of a herptile in order to determine sex is a technique that usually does not work well with adult blue-tongued skinks (although it does seem to work on juveniles). Often you only will end up with a very angry animal.

Blue-tongues will mate in November (assumedly their normal breeding season in the wild) without a cooling period. A cooling period does increase the likelihood of successfully producing young, however.

SEXING

Sexing blue-tongues is a pain. Many breeders have suggested such features as brighter eye color, in juveniles. As a general rule, males are more aggressive than females and more territorial, but females also fight. If two adult blue-tongues are housed together for a short while and are different sexes, the male will tend to chase the female; if two males are housed together, the dominant male will chase the subordinate male. Two females may simply fight or ignore each other. Personally, I think the somewhat swollen tail base housing the male hemipenes seems to work fairly well, though it may not be visible all year.

MATING

If your blue-tongues have been cooled and you have the sexes right, mating behavior should be male becomes much more aggressive, and you will hear bedding and hide tubes being thrown about during the evening hours. He basically is trying to get a grip on the female's side, and he'll grab her tail or legs in the process. If the female is not yet receptive, fighting can get very rough and the animals will have

It is better to place a female blue-tongued skink into a male's enclosure when trying to elicit a mating response. If the reverse is done, it is very possible that no mating will occur. Shown are a pair of New Guinea Blue-tongued Skinks, *Tiliqua gigas*, locked in copulation.

visible within a few hours or days of the skinks being put together. For some reason, if a male is put into the terrarium with a female she is likely to just ignore him and no mating will result. After cooling, it thus is best to put the female into the male's terrarium. If they are ready to breed, the male begins to follow and chase the female, keeping his chin near her rump. After a few days the to be separated for a day or two and tried again. Never leave mating condition skinks together unattended—you'll end up with even more scarring and missing toes than normal. Eventually he is able to clamp his jaws on the female's lower side or nape of the neck and gain leverage to hold her steady and twist her to the side. The tails may twist about each other. At this point he levers his

PHOTO OF *TILIQUA MULTIFASCIATA* BY K. H. SWITAK

Average time of gestation for a blue-tongued skink is somewhere around three to five months. During that time, the gravid female is very likely to have a greatly increased appetite.

cloaca under hers and erects a hemipenis (which appears quite small, more or less smooth, and bright pink) that he inserts into the female's cloaca. (The female correspondingly lifts her tail a bit and also lifts the scales covering the base of the cloaca.) Insemination appears to be accomplished quickly, less than two minutes, but the skinks can hold position for several minutes before separating. The pair may mate several times over a period of a week or two before losing interest. At this point it is best to put the animals in separate terraria.

GESTATION

Pregnant females eat like horses. They need an increased diet with vitamin and mineral supplements and additional calcium. Gestation lasts about three to five months, but very little specific information on variation in the different captive-bred species has been published. As term approaches, the female becomes heavier and heavier but remains active though obviously uncomfortable. Often she stops eating just a week or so before birth. If mating occurs at the beginning of February, then you can expect young sometime between the beginning of May and the end of June. The mother simply drops the babies wherever it is comfortable for her and moves on.

BABIES

As the young are born, they should be carefully removed to separate terraria so they can get individual care and attention from the beginning. There are no indications that the mother will eat her young, but she is a large lizard and could accidentally stomp one into the bedding. Litters are variable in blue-tongues, from only one to three babies in the Shingleback, *Trachydosaurus rugosus*, to as many as 25 in the Northern Blue-tongue, *Tiliqua scincoides intermedia*. Young and small females probably have smaller litters than older, larger females, but most species have babies about 4 to 6 inches long at birth.

The first thing a baby blue-tongue does is eat the afterbirth or placenta. It nibbles the tissue along the blood vessels first and then downs the blood vessels and stem. This likely gives it a boost of hormones and antibodies from the mother and gives it some protection until its own immune system comes into play.

Babies like it a bit warmer than adults, at least for the first six months or so, but otherwise they really are just miniature adults. They bask and then cool down in another section of the terrarium. Help them to develop their personality by regular sessions of handling, but remember that they still are small and rather delicate. Adjust the size and frequency of feedings to their body size and activity. There is no reason to

An albino Common Blue-tongued Skink. As captive-bred blue-tongues become more common, mutations and varieties are sure to appear.

PHOTO BY K. H. SWITAK

PHOTO OF A PINK-TONGUED SKINK BY R. G. SPRACKLAND

Newborns can be cared for much as the adults, one small difference being that they need their enclosure temperature a little higher. Also, they should be kept separate from the adults, who may accidentally trample them or bite them inadvertently.

attempt to cool babies down during the winter until they are fully mature, so don't put them through such stress.

PROFIT POTENTIAL

All the blue-tongued skinks are expensive lizards, and the temptation is to try to breed them as soon and as often as possible to recoup your original expenses. This may not always work, because blue-tongues take quite a while to mature and have rather small litters. If you do succeed in breeding bright, healthy specimens, however, you are almost assured of a market and a decent price because the demand for captive-bred blue-tongues currently exceeds the supply. By the way, there are indications that at least some females give birth only every second year, making it even harder to get babies for the market. You'd be better off just thinking of your blue-tongue as a great pet rather than a source of income, but admittedly there really is a potential for making a few dollars if you are careful, persistent, and lucky.

PHOTO BY K. H. SWITAK

Above: For the sake of conservation, professional breeders should consider propagating some of the lesser-known blue-tongued skinks, like this *Cyclodomorphus branchialis* from southwestern Australia. **Below:** Virtually none of Australia's native herptiles are allowed to be exported from the country. Thus, specimens produced by breeders in other nations often command a very high price. Shown is a mother and two young of the Shingleback Skink, *Trachydosaurus rugosus*, a species almost never seen in the commercial pet trade.

PHOTO BY K. H. SWITAK

OAK SKINKS

RECOGNITION

At first glance the oak skinks, genus *Cyclodomorphus*, bear little resemblance to the blue-tongues. However, they share both the blue tongue (at least in juveniles) and the scalation character of parietal scales separated by an interparietal and not in contact, plus they have the third toe equal in length or a bit longer than the fourth, all characters of the group. Like the Pink-tongued Skink, *Hemisphaeriodon gerrardi*, the tail is about as long as the snout-vent length and breaks easily. The body and head are relatively slender, the neck not especially distinct, and the ear lobules are absent or nearly so, making the skinks appear very much like more typical skinks familiar to most hobbyists. There are only 22 to 28 scales around the body as compared to 30 to 34 in the Pink-tongue, a count that is difficult for the average hobbyist to make. In many ways adult oak skinks look like baby Pink-tongues with reduced patterns, and the two groups certainly are very closely related. They have, in fact, been synonymized by several herpetologists, though many works do retain them as distinct genera.

SPECIES

Because the oak skinks are virtually unknown to American

Although hardly comparable to the blue-tongued skinks at first glance, the oak skinks, genus *Cyclodomorphus*, do in fact share many of the same characteristics, including, in juvenile specimens, a blue tongue. Photo by R. W. Van Devender.

There currently are three species in the genus *Cyclodomorphus*, none of which appear in the herpetological hobby with any great regularity. All occur in Australia and have non-overlapping ranges. The specimens on these pages represent probably undescribed species. Photo by R. W. Van Devender.

and European hobbyists, the three species are easily confused. To an Australian naturalist the species are readily distinguished by distribution, as all three have non-overlapping ranges, but in color pattern and structure they are remarkably alike.

The species with the widest range is the Western Oak Skink, *Cyclodomorphus branchialis* (Guenther, 1867), a small (snout-vent length about 4 inches, total length almost 8 inches), slender,

groove, a short line arcing back from the nostril, that is absent in the Eastern Oak Skink. The color varies considerably from grayish to bright olive-brown, with or without tiny black spots on many of the scales of the back. Babies often have many tiny yellowish spots over the body and tail sometimes arranged in indistinct rows. The lips of adults are pale (though some of the lip scales may have dark edges), as is the belly. Males are said to have gray

ARTWORK BY JOHN R. QUINN

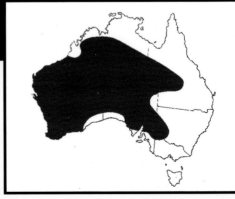

Above: *Cyclodomorphus branchialis.*
Right: Range of *Cyclodomorphus branchialis.*

brownish species with very short legs and a remarkably elongated body. The tail is shorter than the snout-vent length but still quite long and slender. Technically the species is defined by its small size and the presence of a postnarial

throats in contrast to the white throats of females. In some specimens from near Geraldton there are traces of two or three large dark spots on the side of the neck (the "gills" referred to by the species name). Babies have large heads, a feature typical of most blue-tongues, often are brightly

Right: Range of *Cyclodomorphus maxima*. Below: *Cyclodomorphus maxima*.

ARTWORK BY JOHN R. QUINN

patterned, and may have heavily marked lips.

Variation in this species is complicated, and it is likely that it consists of a complex of several species or subspecies. There are differences in size, scale counts, color pattern, and details of foot scalation that need to be examined in great detail. Specimens from Geraldton, for instance, have the distinctive spots on the side of the throat, while those from the very dry spinifex deserts of the southern part of the range away from the coast (once called *melanops*) lack spotting on the belly.

Western Oak Skinks are nocturnal ground-dwellers that feed on a variety of small insects, snails, earthworms, and occasional bits of fruit. They hide under logs, rocks, and leaf litter during the day. Females give birth to two very large young (almost half the length and bulk of the mother). Though the range encompasses much of western and central Australia from western Queensland to South Australia and Western Australia, the species is not evenly distributed, is not conspicuous, and remains rather poorly known. It is presently almost unknown in captivity in the Northern Hemisphere.

Closely related to *Cyclodomorphus branchialis* is the poorly known Kimberley Oak Skink, *C. maxima* Storr, a species described as recently as 1976. It is restricted to a small area of Western Australia in the Kimberley area, where specimens are found in dry forests on sandstone. In all respects it seems to be similar to the Western Oak Skink, but it is twice as large, having a snout-vent length of more than 8 inches. As

recently figured, adults are a pale tan with relatively pale scale centers scattered over the back, especially posteriorly and on the tail. Babies have the characteristic large heads, a pale nape band, and broken pale bands across the back. There may be two or three indistinct black spots on the side of the neck as in some Western Oak Skinks. The postnarial groove is present.

Much more common, at least in nature, is the Eastern Oak or She-Oak Skink, *Cyclodomorphus casuarinae*, of the southeastern

Right: Range of *Cyclodomorphus casuarinae*. Below: *Cyclodomorphus casuarinae*.

ARTWORK BY JOHN R. QUINN

Perhaps the best-known of the oak skinks is the Eastern Oak, or She-Oak, Skink, *Cyclodomorphus casuarinae*. It occurs in large numbers and often around areas heavily developed by man. It is a nocturnal ground-dweller and is largely carnivorous.

corner of Australia and northern Tasmania. This skink often occurs in large numbers in developed areas and is fairly well-known though not exported for the herpetoculture trade. It tends to be a pale brown, slender skink up to 10 inches long (half of this tail). There is a rather complicated color pattern on the back consisting of many pale scale centers and fine dark lines arranged to produce a series of narrow stripes running from the neck to the tail base. Dark scale edges are also well-developed on the sides, appearing as fine broken vertical dark stripes that angle back a bit. There may be a dark teardrop below the eye. The belly is pale with dark scale edges that produce vague bands. Babies are said to have a broad dark brown, almost blackish, band across the nape. Overall the Eastern Oak Skink looks a lot like a small Pink-tongued Skink with a poorly developed pattern.

Like the Western Oak Skink, this species is a nocturnal ground-dweller that occurs in dry forests and fields. It can be found under logs and leaf litter during the day, coming out at night to feed on the usual insects, snails, and earthworms. Up to six young have been recorded in a litter, but two or three probably is a more common number. Like the other oak skinks, this species has little record of life in captivity and currently appears to be unavailable to the average hobbyist.

CULTURE

Because of their small size, ground-dwelling habits, and nocturnal activity, oak skinks can be kept much like *Eumeces* and other common hobby skinks. Provide a 20-gallon terrarium with a rather dry substrate and a patch of moister peat moss. Pieces of cork bark and similar cover will be used by the skinks during the day. Temperatures of about 80°F should suffice. Little is known about captive-breeding in this genus, but at least the Eastern Oak Skink should profit from a short cooling period. Certainly these are the least known of the blue-tongues and the least spectacular. Until they become generally available it is hard to tell if they have a future in the hobby or not.

PINK-TONGUES

RECOGNITION

The only species currently recognized in the genus *Hemisphaeriodon* is *H. gerrardi* (Gray, 1825), a fascinating and very different species of blue-tongue. Like the oak skinks, the Pink-tongued Skink is relatively slender and has a long tail that instantly distinguishes it from the true blue-tongues. In most specimens the tail is at least as long as the snout-vent length and may be almost 1.5 times as long. It is slender and fully prehensile, able to easily wrap around branches and fingers. The legs are long and strong, with long toes much like those of a normal skink, but with the third toe equal

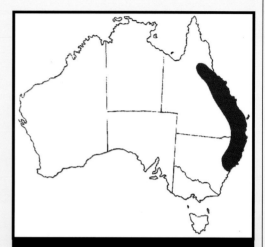

Above: Range of *Hemisphaeriodon gerrardi*. Below: Although once considered part of *Tiliqua*, the Pink-tongued Skink, *Hemisphaeriodon gerrardi*, has since been placed in its own monotypic genus. Characteristics that separate it from *Tiliqua* include a long tail and strongly arboreal habits.

PHOTO BY R. D. BARTLETT

to the fourth or slightly longer (remember, the fourth toe is longer than the third in most skinks). The leg and tail development are adaptations for the lizard's tendency to climb in search of insect and snail prey, for unlike the other blue-tongues *H. gerrardi* is not an especially terrestrial species.

Hemisphaeriodon gerrardi has the large, boxy head typical of blue-tongues and the slender neck that allows it free movement. The body is more slender than that of the true blue-tongues, more like that of the oak skinks. There are differences in head scalation from other blue-tongues, but few are of any consequence to the hobbyist. The large, bright pink tongue is startling and one of the more appealing aspects of the lizard. Pink-tongues share with the oak skinks the habit of tongue flicking, constantly moving the tongue in and out to "sense" the ground and surroundings, a habit not typical of the true blue-tongues. Coloration is interesting in the Pink-tongue but not really bright. Most specimens are a pale gray to very pale tan with six to eight brown bands across the back, the bands varying greatly in width from narrow to quite wide. Usually the bands angle backward low on the sides and, if wide enough, may show traces of a pale stripe within the dark brown. Band width and color seem to vary individually, and narrow-banded mothers may give birth to broad-banded young. The tail also is banded, while the belly scales are tinged with brownish.

PHOTO BY PAUL FREED

Aren't Pink-tongued Skinks supposed to have pink tongues? Well, yes, but only as adults. As juveniles, their tongues are as blue as those possessed by specimens of the genus *Tiliqua*.

There is a distinctive head pattern in many specimens consisting of a broad dark brown teardrop below the eye continuing over the jaws and across the throat; occasionally the teardrop is absent or there are two or three dark bands across the throat.

NATURAL HISTORY

Though a large skink, 8 inches in body length and with a tail at least as long, for a total length of 16 to 20 inches, the Pink-tongue always appears slender and more agile than true blue-tongues. It has invaded a niche with a bit less competition than the ground-dwelling *Tiliqua* and has become a nocturnal (night-active) or crepuscular (active at dusk and dawn) hunter of snails, slugs, and insects. Though often active during the daytime as well, it is most comfortable when the sun is set and the snails come out to play. Also unlike more common blue-tongues, it is a creature of

Behaviorally the Pink-tongue spends the day in seclusion under logs and litter, coming out when the sun goes down. The long legs and prehensile tail allow it to climb in low shrubs looking for snails, its preferred food. When snails are found they are grabbed in the

Keeping a Pink-tongued Skink is not particularly difficult. The animal will require a semi-humid enclosure with plenty of plants and climbing branches, plus a diet of both animal and plant matter.

PHOTO OF A JUVENILE BY W. P. MARA

the wet forests, from true rainforest to seasonally dry woodlands. Native only to a rather narrow strip along the central East Coast of Australia from near Sydney to the southern Cape York Peninsula, it has a relatively small range for a blue-tongue and must be suffering somewhat from loss of habitat to human development. Its moist subtropical habitat must be remembered when the skink is kept in captivity, as we will see shortly.

strong jaws and beat against a branch or rock until the shell cracks, when they are gulped down. Insects are treated in much the same manner. Populations are sparsely distributed through the range, and Pink-tongues are never especially common lizards. Mating follows the typical behavior for the blue-tongues, with a male following a selected female, perhaps for days, until she is ready to mate. He grabs her with his jaws near the nape or behind a front leg and twists his body and tail about hers until the cloacas are in contact and a hemipenis can be inserted. Gestation takes about five months and results in a litter of about two dozen young that are 4 inches long.

CULTURE

You shouldn't try to keep Pink-tongued Skinks as you would the more common blue-tongues from dry habitats. This skink needs a taller terrarium with an assortment of climbing branches and a well- but since they prefer a well-planted terrarium the plants need good light to survive. Provide two or more hide boxes for the skink, making sure they are partially embedded in the substrate so the lizard can get away from the light if it prefers. A basking light focused on some flat rocks still is a good idea, and most Pink-tongues will learn to adjust their schedule to match that of their owner. With a bit of effort on your part the skink will learn to come out when the

PHOTO BY PAUL FREED

Pink-tongues are among the easier-to-breed tiliquine skinks. One advantage they offer to a commercial breeder is a relatively large number of newborns per litter—a dozen or more is not unusual.

secured lid to prevent escapes. Temperatures in the bedding of about 75°F are suitable, with air temperatures a bit less, both dropping by up to 15° at night. The lizards are most active at night so really have little need of lighting, lights go on but still will feed in the dark. The terrarium should be more moist than usual for blue-tongues, but well ventilated to prevent fungus and condensation. Daily spraying with warm water will keep the cage moist enough and also help the plants.

Though it prefers snails, slugs, and insects as food, Pink-tongues also will take sweet fruits such as melon and banana and occasionally will snack on veggies. They can be taught to take snails from the fingers, always a neat trick to observe. (Caution: The jaws are strong and accidents such as bad aim can happen.) Though

sometimes can be a problem), they will reach full maturity in about 30 months. A cooling period like that for most blue-tongues aids breeding, but of course lower temperatures are necessary before the lizards cease feeding. Also as usual, the sexes appear to be almost impossible to distinguish externally and are best told apart by how they act

PHOTO BY R. D. BARTLETT

Getting a newborn Pink-tongued Skink to sexual maturity will take about 30 months of good care. The only problem a keeper may have is with occasionally providing snails as a part of their diet; these seem to be their favorite food item.

many individuals are not choosy about food, some may insist on having strange foods rubbed over a snail. Captive-bred young can be adapted to the usual dog food diet but always prefer live foods.

Baby Pink-tongues usually have blue tongues that change color with age, soon becoming the bright pink typical of the species. (Occasional adults retain the juvenile blue tongue.) Because the litters are large (often a dozen or more), these skinks are fairly easy to produce in some numbers in captivity, though they still are not common or cheap. The young, as usual, should be removed to individual terraria and kept fairly moist. If they feed well (which

when ready to breed.

Pink-tongued Skinks currently are the least expensive of the blue-tongues to purchase, at least when captive-bred babies are available. They are far from common in the hobby, however, and all stock must be captive-bred because of Australian export regulations. Resemblances between the Pink-tongue and the Solomons Monkey Skink (*Corucia*) are obvious, with the two species being kept in very similar fashion, though Pink-tongues are much easier to keep than Monkey Skinks. This species deserves more attention from hobbyists and more attempts at large-scale breeding.

TRUE BLUE-TONGUES

RECOGNITION

No hobbyist should have a problem recognizing the members of the genus *Tiliqua*, the "true" blue-tongued skinks. This genus contains the most familiar species in the hobby at the moment as well as the largest and heaviest skinks always slender and pointed, never broad and blunt.

All the species of *Tiliqua* are livebearers, and all are active during the day. Of course all the species (except *T. adelaidensis*) have bright blue tongues that contrast against bright pink fleshy

PHOTO BY R. D. BARTLETT

Skinks of the genus *Tiliqua* are more common in private collections than members of the other tiliquine genera. Distinctive characteristics include smooth or only slightly folded scales and a tail that is slender and pointed.

next to the Solomons Monkey Skink (*Corucia*). The genus is quite uniform in body shape and scalation and is closely related to the Shingleback, *Trachydosaurus*, which appears to be derived from some *Tiliqua* species with very little change in its molecular biology. *Tiliqua* differs from *Cyclodomorphus* and *Hemisphaeriodon* by its shorter tail, which is never more than 75% of the snout-vent length and often only 50%. The toes are relatively short, the third equal to or longer than the length of the fourth. From *Trachydosaurus*, the true blue-tongues differ obviously in having smooth or only weakly striated (folded) scales and all the head scales distinct and in regular patterns. The tail of *Tiliqua* is

mouth interiors. Blue-tongues and the Shingleback share a defensive behavior when threatened by a snake or mammal predator: they curl the body so the tail lies next to the head and open the mouth wide while hissing loudly. The combination of sound, brilliant mouth colors, and widened, almost circular body outline is enough to deter most small predators, and the skinks have strong jaw muscles and heavy teeth to back up the bite that follows if the predator persists. Owners should be sure to handle their blue-tongues frequently to keep them tame, but remember to always be gentle: the bite can be ferocious if a skink feels it is threatened or hurt.

Currently six species of *Tiliqua* are recognized, one with an additional described subspecies (plus a perhaps undescribed subspecies). The species fall into two groups on the basis of an easily seen scalation character: in *T. scincoides* and *T. gigas*, which are quite similar in general appearance, the anterior temporal scales (the second row behind the eyes) are elongated and obviously different from the row of rather squarish scales (posterior temporals) behind them. In the other *Tiliqua* species the anterior temporals and posterior temporals are similar in size and shape, rather squarish or short

rectangular. It is easy to see head scales in these big lizards. All the species are easily distinguished by color pattern and size. The following brief key should help.

DWARF BLUE-TONGUED SKINK: *TILIQUA ADELAIDENSIS*

This, the smallest of the true blue-tongues, was described by Peters in 1863 and has always been the rarest and least-known species of the genus. Known from a few areas around Adelaide, South Australia, the species was thought to be extinct and had not been seen for many years, but it was

1A. Anterior temporals elongated relative to posterior temporals; back with at least six narrow brown to blackish bands 2

1B. Anterior temporals squarish, not obviously different from posterior temporals; back variously colored 3

2A. Sides between legs pale, crossed at least partially by alternating dark and pale bars; legs usually pale .... Common Blue-tongued Skink

2B. Sides between legs dark, often blackish, crossed by at most vaguely defined brownish bands; legs back above .... New Guinea Blue-tongued Skink

3A. Back without strong crossbands, instead mottled or blotched light on dark 4

3B. Back with distinct dark

crossbands 5

4A. Adults less than 7 inches long; back almost unicolored, with very narrow and indistinct dark crosslines; tail over 50% snout-vent length .... Dwarf Blue-tongued Skink

4B. Adults more than 14 inches long; back dark with pale, regularly arranged blotches; tail 50% or less of snout-vent length .... Blotched Blue-tongued Skink

5A. Back with nine or more narrow brown crossbands on a grayish background; body often appears grossly flattened and inflated .... Centralian Blue-tongued Skink

5B. Back with five or six very broad brown crossbands on a creamish background; body not exceptionally inflated or flattened .... Western Blue-tongued Skink

rediscovered in several small populations in 1992.

Unlike any other *Tiliqua*, the Dwarf is small (maximum snout-vent length only 3.5 inches, with a tail as much as 75% of the snout-vent length) and lacks a distinctive color pattern on the back. Instead, the back is reddish brown with narrow black lines marking the edges of the scale rows. There may be a weak or strongly defined row of small black flecks or blotches down the center of the back. The feet often are more golden brown than the back. This pattern probably is one of camouflage or disruption, allowing it to blend into the dry scrub plains covered with tussock grasses, where it is active during the day and retires at night to burrows made by large spiders. It feeds on the usual insects such as caterpillars and grasshoppers and also eats fruits and greens like most other blue-tongues. This is a very sedentary species that seldom ventures far from its burrow even to chase prey.

The Dwarf Blue-tongued Skink, *Tiliqua adelaidensis*, is considered the rarest and least studied member of the blue-tongues. It was described back in 1863 and still is known only from a few locations near Adelaide, South Australia.

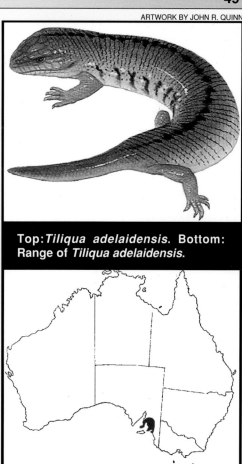

Top:*Tiliqua adelaidensis*. Bottom: Range of *Tiliqua adelaidensis*.

Not too much is as yet known of its reproduction, but males are in breeding condition in the Southern Hemisphere spring and at that time wander around quite a bit. Young are born in the female's burrow during February and March, the Australian late summer to autumn. One to four young comprise a litter. The Dwarf Blue-tongued Skink is being kept in several zoos and may eventually turn into a fairly well-known animal that has come back from the brink of extinction.

NEW GUINEA BLUE-TONGUED SKINK: *TILIQUA GIGAS*

When Schneider described *Tiliqua gigas* in 1801, he though the specimen came from Egypt or the Ural Mountains of Russia, a type of error not uncommon at this time, when species were described from single specimens brought

PHOTO BY R. D. BARTLETT

The New Guinea Blue-tongued Skink, *Tiliqua gigas*, is one of the stouter, more powerfully built members of its genus, which is something a keeper should remember when handling adult specimens. Claws can be sharp, and bites can be very painful.

back to Europe by sailors and soldiers, or just paintings by amateur artists. Actually, the New Guinea Blue-tongue has a broad range from southern New Guinea (including the D'Entrecasteaux Group at the southeast) west through the various Indonesian islands (including at least some of the Moluccas) and supposedly to Sumatra, producing the largest range of any species of the genus and the only one to extend widely outside Australia. It inhabits scrubland, especially on the small islands, and is truly a subtropical species with rather low humidity requirements, as might not be expected from the general range. This is a big (20 inches), bulky species with short but strong legs and, if need be, a strong bite. Some people consider it one of the dullest blue-tongues because the body is basically a golden to grayish brown with darker brown crossbands (about seven, give or take a couple) continued onto the tail. The sides are covered with a broad, irregular blackish brown band that extends over the legs and is occasionally interrupted by weak extensions of the golden brown back color onto the side. The belly is pale with many dusky spots at the edges of the scales. There may or may not be a dark stripe behind the eye. Males seem to be a bit heavier and duller than females, possibly with

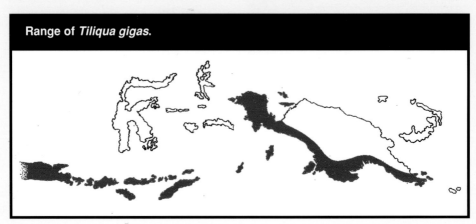

Range of *Tiliqua gigas*.

somewhat shorter tails. At least some males have the head and body scales strongly ridged or folded. The eyes are reddish brown to bright red, variable with season and mood.

This species can be kept like typical blue-tongues, doing well at a terrarium temperature of 75 to 80°F, dropping to the 60's at night. An area under a basking light should be considerably warmer, 90°F or more. They disappear into the bedding or their hide tubes during the dark period, coming out to bask and be handled and fondled when their keeper comes home. They can be skittish but soon adapt. Imported as young adults, often only 12 to 14 inches total length, they continue to grow at a good rate on a diet of dog food supplemented with fruits and veggies, plus the occasional live insect tidbit. Mating is vigorous, to say the least, so expect females to be scarred and perhaps missing a toe or two. Gestation lasts about four to five months, with litters of 10 to 15 to be expected. Maturity takes about two years in captivity, probably longer in nature.

This personable species still is

PHOTO BY AARON NORMAN

The New Guinea Blue-tongued Skink is an easy captive, requiring a daytime temperature of around 75 to 80°F/24 to 26°C (with a 90°F/32°C basking spot) and a diet consisting of mostly animal material with some vegetables thrown in.

imported from Indonesian regions of New Guinea and the islands to the west, usually as young adults a bit over a foot long. Because they are wild, they should be vetted and treated for worms. They must be handled regularly to become tame, otherwise you could end up with a scratching, biting monster. Males are very aggressive, so caution is advised. A few captive-bred young are becoming available currently. One of the least expensive blue-tongues, it definitely deserves more attention from hobbyists and breeders.

CENTRALIAN BLUE-TONGUED SKINK: *TILIQUA MULTIFASCIATA*

Found over virtually all the dry northwestern and north-central part of Australia, the Centralian Blue-tongue was first described by Sternfeld in 1919 and has never been common in the hobby. In many ways it looks like a dull Common Blue-tongue, being grayish above with many (often 10 to 12) narrow orangish brown crossbands that may be broken and irregular. There is a broad black stripe back from the eye (the temporal stripe) as in many large blue-tongues. The first impression

PHOTO BY K. H. SWITAK

Left: Since the Centralian Blue-tongued Skink, *Tiliqua multifasciata*, is a creature of dry desert regions, its surroundings in captivity also must be dry. A sandy substrate with a daytime temperature of around 85°F/30°C (with a 95°F/35°C basking spot) will suffice. Right: Range of *Tiliqua multifasciata*.

on seeing a Centralian Blue-tongue is that something is wrong with the lizard. It is distinctly flattened and very broad, making it look grossly fat or extremely pregnant. When facing an attacker it puffs up even more and looks even broader. At about 16 to 18 inches in total length, with a correspondingly large head, it is a lizard to be remembered.

Its habitat is the dry, often stony plains and deserts typical of northwestern Australia, so it obviously does not need humid surroundings in the terrarium. It likes warm basking areas and relatively limited temperature drops at night (about 95°F under the basking light during the day, 75°F in the burrows at night). Only recently has this species appeared in small numbers in the herp hobby, and it draws big prices. A litter consists of about ten youngsters much like the mother in appearance, just a bit more

slender and with the relatively larger head characteristic of most baby blue-tongues. Its odd appearance is sure to make it a desirable lizard when it becomes more readily available.

BLOTCHED BLUE-TONGUED SKINK: *TILIQUA NIGROLUTEA*

Perhaps the most spectacularly colored blue-tongue, the Blotched has been known for almost two centuries, being described by Quoy

The Blotched Blue-tongued Skink, *Tiliqua nigrolutea*, once was fairly common in the herpetocultural hobby, but these days it is quite scarce, so obtaining a specimen may be difficult.

PHOTO BY H. HANSEN

and Gaimard in 1824. Restricted to southeastern Australia and Tasmania, it inhabits many different types of habitats from coastal forest to dry plains and thus is very adaptable as far as temperature and humidity requirements go. The back is bright

Right: Range of *Tiliqua nigrolutea*. Below: The Blotched Blue-tongue occurs in a variety of habitats and thus is highly adaptable in captivity as far as housing is concerned.

PHOTO BY H. HANSEN

pinkish to salmon-cream in color, overlain with irregular bright chocolate to blackish brown bands that run both from head to tail and from side to side. The brown bands isolate irregular blotches of the pale background color, producing the characteristic blotched pattern that makes this lizard so distinctive. Additionally, the lower sides (and belly in young) are covered with an open network of brown to produce a reticulated pattern unique in the genus. The

tail is ringed in brown, and the dark bar behind the eye is poorly developed or absent. At 14 to 16 inches in total length this is a medium-sized blue-tongue, but it is quite bulky and at first glance appears larger than it really is.

Once seen fairly often in the hobby, and still illustrated in almost any book on hobby lizards, the Blotched Blue-tongue today is rare and virtually unobtainable by the average hobbyist. It seldom has been bred, but is known to produce a litter of eight to ten young about 6 inches long after a four- or five-month gestation period. It is very tolerant of terrarium temperature extremes and prefers temperatures a bit cooler than those for the Common Blue-tongue. A winter cooling period may be necessary to promote breeding in the terrarium; southeastern Australia has quite cold winters. Feeding and mating behavior are as usual for the genus. If available more regularly and at lower prices it would be a premium hobby blue-tongue, but for the moment it is a rarity for only the elite keepers and breeders.

WESTERN BLUE-TONGUED SKINK: *TILIQUA OCCIPITALIS*

Western Blue-tongues, first described by Peters in 1863, might more appropriately be called "southern blue-tongues" because they range across most of southern Australia from Shark Bay, Western Australia, to western New South Wales. It is a lizard of very dry, often desert, habitats, and thus can take warm daytime temperatures and very low humidities. I think it is one of the prettiest blue-tongues, being basically a yellowish tan lizard with four to six very wide, bright, pale

brown bands on the body and sometimes extending well onto the white belly. The top of the head is pale brown, and there is a broad black streak behind the eye. The tail is contrastingly ringed in bright brown and cream. Closely related to the Centralian Blue-tongue, which occurs to the north of its range,

ARTWORK BY JOHN R. QUINN

Tiliqua occipitalis.

it lacks the distorted appearance of that species and appears rather elegant. The total length may exceed 18 inches.

This pretty species appears to be unavailable to hobbyists at the moment, being protected from export by Australian regulations. It has no history in herpetoculture, unfortunately, and its natural and terrarium histories are almost

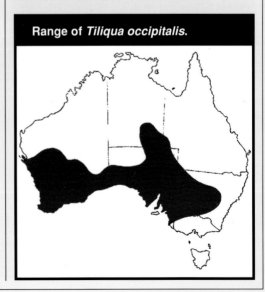
Range of *Tiliqua occipitalis.*

unknown. We can only hope that the coming years will lead to at least a few Western Blue-tongues appearing in the hobby, though of course prices will be very high. It gives you something to look forward to!

COMMON BLUE-TONGUED SKINK: *TILIQUA SCINCOIDES*

Australian herp literature calls this species the Eastern Blue-tongue, but hobbyists tend to distinguish between the two subspecies by different common names (Eastern Blue-tongue for *T.*

PHOTO BY K. H. SWITAK

The Northern Blue-tongued Skink, *Tiliqua scincoides intermedia*, is popular with hobbyists and makes a good captive in spite of its need for a super-hot basking spot (often as high as 105°F/41°C).

scincoides scincoides from southern and eastern Australia, and Northern Blue-tongue for *T. scincoides intermedia* from northern Australia), so it seems appropriate to give the species as a whole a different common name. Of course this is the most common blue-tongue in captivity, with captive-bred young and adults of both the Australian subspecies readily available if you have the money—this is not a cheap lizard even if it is common. It has been known for over two centuries, being described by White in 1790, making it the

first described blue-tongue, and is widely distributed over many different habitats in Australia, from rather moist forests to dry plains. This is the typical day-active, heat-loving blue-tongue, needing very high body temperatures (as much as 105°F, and certainly not below 90°F) before it can become active and digest food. This need for heat must be reflected in adequate basking lights in any Common Blue-tongue terrarium.

As might be expected from the existence of subspecies, this species is quite variable in details of color, but it always is creamy tan or pale

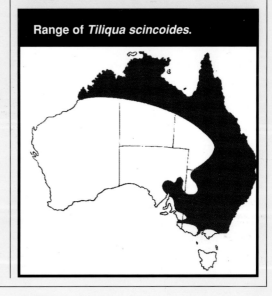

Range of *Tiliqua scincoides*.

golden tan above and below with about eight rather narrow darker crossbands over the back. The head is pale golden tan above with white lips, the belly is white, sometimes with traces of the dark crossbands from the back extending over it, and the tail is ringed in bright brown and whitish. The legs are pale to dark brown above but never black. There usually is a blackish brown elongated to squarish spot over the base of the front leg. Average adults are 18 to 24 inches long (the tail often equal to about half to three-quarters the snout-vent length); there are records of captive-bred and raised adults approaching 30 inches overall, a truly gigantic size for a skink.

Presently three subspecies are recognized by hobbyists, two from Australia and one recently imported from Irian Jaya (the Indonesian or western portion of the island of New Guinea, which permits animal exports; the Australian-related country occupying the eastern portion of the island is properly called

PHOTO BY K. H. SWITAK

If you can afford it, purchase specimens of *Tiliqua scincoides* that were cultured in captivity. Some commercial adult specimens may be the product of illegal smuggling and importation

Papua New Guinea, and presently it does not allow exports).

The form from southern and eastern Australia, the Eastern Blue-tongue, *Tiliqua scincoides scincoides*, is very variable in details of color and pattern, some specimens being very bright and others quite dull. However, it usually has a distinct black or dark brown streak back from the eye and has the brown bands of the back extending over the sides, angling slightly backward, and often continuing well onto the belly. Adults seldom exceed 20 to 22 inches in total length. Captive-bred specimens are common (in fact, as with most other Australian lizards, wild-caught specimens are likely to be black-market contraband smuggled out of the country) but fairly expensive, especially the more brightly colored adults; babies are affordable if you have a large hobby budget.

The Northern Blue-tongue, *Tiliqua scincoides intermedia*, obviously from the drier northern portion of Australia, is paler and brighter in color than the Eastern. First, it lacks the dark stripe back from the eye and often has the black blotch over the front leg reduced in size. The bands across the back may be quite irregular, with many white scales in them, but the dark bands usually turn nearly black on the upper sides and are separated there by orange to bright golden tan bars. The lower sides are white and not

and adjacent islands. In many respects it looks like a cross between the Northern and Eastern Blue-tongues, lacking the dark eye stripe like the Northern but having the dark bands of the back extending low onto the sides and often onto the belly. It seems amazing that this large (20 to 22 inches) skink was not discovered until 1990 or so, and its status remains undetermined. It has

PHOTO BY K. H. SWITAK

A nice feature of *Tiliqua scincoides* is the fact that many specimens are quite docile and thus require little or no handling in order to calm down. *Scincoides* is the blue-tongue species most often kept by hobbyists.

crossed by the bands from the back. This form grows larger than the Eastern, commonly reaching 25 inches in captivity, with records to 30 inches. Common in captivity and greatly desired by breeders and average hobbyists alike, it is moderately expensive when sold as babies.

The Irian Jaya Blue-tongue, *Tiliqua scincoides* subsp., appears to be found in southern Irian Jaya

been suggested that it is a valid but undescribed subspecies or full species, but the possibility remains that it really is a cultivated cross of the two Australian subspecies with incorrect locality data, transshipped through Irian Jaya to "legalize" black-market Australian lizards. Perhaps by the time you read this its status will have been determined. Currently it is expensive and seldom available as captive-bred specimens.

Recently a second "undescribed" Irian Jaya blue-tongue has been imported, this one a bright golden brown animal with narrow dark bars over the back and mostly black legs. In many respects it looks like a cross between *T. gigas* and *T. scincoides intermedia*, but again its true status is presently unknown. Still another recent Irian Jaya import, called the Tanimbar Blue-tongue, bears a striking similarity to *T. occipitalis*. You could almost get the feeling that

species and probably have been continuously available to hobbyists for over 50 years. Their care was covered in an earlier chapter, though it must be repeated that these lizards need more heat to become active and stay healthy than do the other commonly kept species. Provide strong basking lights most of the day as well as one or two undertank heaters, but also be sure there is a cool corner of the cage for the lizard to retire to. Eastern Blue-tongues generally are less snappy than

A lot of "oddball" *Tiliqua scincoides* forms currently are being imported from Irian Jaya and other places and could be the products of large-scale hybridization on lizard farms. When purchasing a specimen, find out as much about its pedigree as you can.

many of these "new" forms are simply the result of massive hybridization of several *Tiliqua* being kept in lizard farms in Irian Jaya. Only studies of their molecular biology (which can detect hybridization) will provide a final answer to the problem. Buyers should exercise caution before spending large sums on "new" blue-tongues. Breeding hybrids probably will yield only "mutts" rather than beautiful and distinctive animals.

Common Blue-tongues have been kept longer than most of the other

Northerns and are considered to be better pets by many. Some Easterns are quite docile among themselves and can be kept safely in small colonies. Gestation takes the usual four or five months, leading to litters of from 15 to 25 babies up to 7 inches long, number and size depending somewhat on the size of the female. The Irian Jaya Blue-tongue seems to have smaller litters of large-headed young, only 5 to 15, but so far there is little herpetocultural experience with the form.

SHINGLEBACKS

RECOGNITION

Certainly the most unusual blue-tongue is the Shingleback or Bobtail, *Trachydosaurus rugosus* Gray, 1825. One of the more abundant lizards over dry interior eastern Australia and the southern coastal strip west to Shark Bay, it is absent from the highly populated southeastern coast and all of northern Australia. The generic status of this species long has been controversial, and many leading herpetologists would prefer to see it as just another species of *Tiliqua*. A nearly equal number, however, feel it represents a distinct genus, an opinion followed here. Though obviously very closely related to the true blue-tongues (studies of its molecular chemistry indicate it has deviated little from *Tiliqua* species at the molecular level), it has numerous differences in scalation and body form that allow it to be recognized instantly. It does, however, bear some resemblance to *Tiliqua nigrolutea*, the Blotched Blue-tongue.

This is the shortest-tailed blue-tongue, with the broad, usually very blunt tail being only a quarter of the snout-vent length and much like the head at first glance. (An apparently undescribed subspecies of Shingleback has a distinctly pointed tail and may mark a transition to *Tiliqua* species.) The scales of the body and tail are very large, knobby, and rough, accentuating the resemblance to a pinecone. The hind feet have especially short, thick toes with divided lamellae underneath (a minor but consistent difference from *Tiliqua*). The tongue, as usual, is bright blue in strong contrast to a deep pink background. The scales of the head are greatly fragmented and irregular, making them hard to

PHOTO BY K. H. SWITAK

One of the most interesting and most common (but currently very difficult to obtain privately) blue-tongues is the Shingleback Skink, *Trachydosaurus rugosus*. While studies of the animal's molecular chemistry suggest it to be virtually identical to members of the genus *Tiliqua*, many taxonomists, including the author of this book, feel it belongs in its own genus.

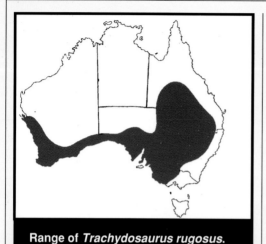

Range of *Trachydosaurus rugosus*.

compare with the more regular scales of the other blue-tongues, another point of contrast, as is the absence of projecting scales (lobules) at the anterior border of the ear openings (present in most true blue-tongues). Maximum length for the species is about 14 to 16 inches, so it is one of the smaller blue-tongue species though certainly the bulkiest.

Coloration varies greatly in the Shingleback. Many specimens are brown or reddish brown with few to many irregular whitish to yellowish spots scattered over the body. Some are entirely brown, while others (especially of the western Australian subspecies *T. r. rugosus*) have the white spots connected into nearly continuous pale bands over the back. Three subspecies are distinguished on differences of form and coloration: *T. r. rugosus* of western Australia has a moderately long and often comparatively slender tail and is heavily spotted or even banded with white; *T. r. konowi* of Rottnest Island, Western Australia, is small and very dark, being uniformly gray with many tiny white specks over the back and belly; and *T. r. asper* of eastern Australia, the form with the shortest, widest, most head-like tail, the most fragmented scalation, and also the

PHOTO BY SUZANNE L. AND JOSEPH T. COLLINS

The Shingleback Skink has large knobby scales on the head and tail, giving it a vague resemblance to a pine cone. Thus, it should come as no surprise that one of its other common names is the Pinecone Skink.

one most likely to be solid brown with no pattern. *T. r. asper* occurs westward to Caiguna and Rawlinna, Western Australia, while *T. r. rugosus* occurs west of a line from Balladonia to Zanthus, Western Australia. An apparently undescribed subspecies (one with a longer, narrower, more pointed tail) occurs north of the Murchison River in Western Australia.

NATURAL HISTORY

A species of dry plains and woodlands, the Shingleback forms colonies of numerous animals in suitable habitats. Animals are relatively sedentary, though in the spring of the year adults tend to wander from one territory to another. In one study, many adults were retaken within 100 yards of the original point repeatedly over six years. The typical Shingleback feeds heavily on local fruits and flowers as well as snails, earthworms, and insects. It also will take carrion and small birds and mammals if it can get them. Its daily routine is like that of other blue-tongues, with a warming period in the morning followed by active feeding and continued basking, then sheltering under logs, litter, or debris as the temperatures drop in late day and night. In nature mating occurs from September through November (southern spring), with one to three young being born during February or March (late southern summer into autumn), a gestation period of about four to five months. Shinglebacks weigh about 50 to 80 grams at birth and, because they are born just before the onset of southern winter, gain very little weight until the following spring. Surviving their first winter after having very little time to feed must be stressful, and there are thought to be high juvenile mortality rates during their first winter. The young also are more subject to predation from both natural marsupial and snake predators and introduced cats and foxes. Even adult skinks must be preyed upon by these same feral introductions.

Mating is typical of the group, with males in nature following females for several days before enticing them to mate. Somewhat long-term pairs may be formed that last for a few mating seasons, but equally often females mate with several males and vice

PHOTO BY R. G. SPRACKLAND

Shinglebacks are calm, resigning creatures that usually don't mind being handled. Since they are creatures of dry regions, they require a very dry enclosure with a warm basking spot.

In spite of the fact that the captive-longevity record for a Shingleback Skink is over 35 years, most live about 12 to 15. As with any other herptile, however, they need their keeper's time and attention or they'll die within a matter of weeks or months!

versa. Maturity seems to be reached at an age of about 30 months, and females are sexually active in nature for at least eight or nine years. Wild specimens seem to live to at least nine or ten years of age, but there is a record of a specimen in England (known as "Stumpy," a great pet and especially fond of bananas) still living and healthy at an age of 35. Average captive longevity seems to be closer to 12 to 15 years, however.

CULTURE

Captive care is relatively simple and doesn't deviate from that for the group as a whole. Make sure the terrarium never becomes too moist (remember that the skinks are from dry areas). A winter cooling is natural for this species and shouldn't be stressful for healthy adults. It eats a variety of plants and invertebrates, as well as the usual dog food basic diet and the occasional pinkie mouse. Mating successes have been low, but because of export restrictions the species has been practically absent from the hobby in America and Europe until recently. A few breeders now have these very expensive lizards and are trying to produce more, but at only one to three young per litter it obviously will be a long time before there are enough specimens to satisfy the demand. Because of its hardiness and tameness (being colonial, several specimens can be kept together with few problems) it would be the best blue-tongue for herpetoculture, if only it were more available.

By the way, literature on the skink in Australia indicates that the sexes are impossible to determine accurately by using external features. Some breeders feel that males have somewhat narrower and more pointed tails than females, but this does not appear to be the case in wild populations of the eastern Australian subspecies. Many of the specimens in captivity seem to be the more brightly colored western subspecies, so perhaps the tail differences noted by breeders work with that subspecies only. If and when more specimens become available it might be possible to accurately sex them afterall.

THE FUTURE OF THE BLUE-TONGUES

Does the future hold great surprises when it comes to hobby blue-tongues? Well, if several

blue-tongues at the moment) might change abruptly with a new political administration. Hobbyists and breeders must work to be sure that there are good numbers of all available species in captivity at all times and that the various lines are not allowed to degenerate. I'm not aware of any legitimate hybridizing experiments being done on blue-tongues (except for one strange colony of *Tiliqua gigas* by *Egernia*

PHOTO BY ISABELLE FRANCAIS

How does the future look for blue-tongued skinks? It's hard to say. If captive-breeding efforts don't increase, more wild specimens may start turning up in the pet shops, which may be great for hobbyists but disastrous for the animals. Only time will tell for sure.

seemingly distinct forms can be discovered in exportable quantities in a fairly well-known area, then the possibility of other new forms from the rest of New Guinea must not be neglected. Additionally, there are signs that Australia may be loosening its strict no-export policies a bit, and new bloodlines of established species, as well as stock of such rarities as the oak skinks and the Western Blue-tongue, might eventually enter the hobby legally even if only in small quantities.

Blue-tongues are one of those groups whose hobby future depends almost entirely on captive-breeding, as export laws of Irian Jaya (the only legal exporter of

cunninghami hybrids in South Africa), and I certainly hope that none will ever affect hobby animals. If you get one or more blue-tongues be sure you try to establish a breeding colony even if you have to borrow a specimen of the opposite sex or loan your specimen out for breeding in exchange for young. Hobbyists must do their part to make sure that blue-tongues, especially the desirable *Tiliqua* species, stay in the hobby forever.

The author will provide bibliographic assistance to interested hobbyists who wish to contact him through T.F.H. Publications.

SUGGESTED READING

RE-110   RE-107   RE-109   RE-124

RE-103   RE-108   RE-101   RE-106

RE-127   RE-112   RE-113   RE-104

RE-102   RE-131   RE-128   RE-136